STUDY OF IMPACT OF FOREX & FIIs

IN S&P CNX DEFTY

Dr. Nisar Munshi

Associate Professor

Institute of Management Studies

JUNAGADH

PREFACE

Real and proper learning comes out of experience and observation. Practical knowledge is one of the best types of learning that one can keep with him up during entire life. Only theoretical aspects of management do not give real corporate knowledge. The main objective of practical training is to develop practical knowledge and awareness about industrial environment in context with theoretical studies of administration and management in specific areas like marketing, finance, HR, production.

The impacts of foreign exchange rate & FIIs in stock market have numerous practical business implications. If international diversification strategies are to be successful, these markets should display low levels of correlation. In addition, understanding the determinants of asset volatilities, as well as their international correlations, are important parameters for the day to day risk management of financial institutions, the risk management of firms operating internationally, and the pricing of contingent claims. This project examines whether there is a impact of exchange rate & FIIs in stock market volatility and correlations. We find that the connection between exchange rates & FIIs in stock market correlations and volatilities are existing in India.

TABLE OF CONTENTS

LIST OF TABLES

LIST OF CHART

PART – 1 GENERAL INFORMATION

1.1 OVERVIEW OF WORLD MARKET

Update November 1, 2007:

Well, glad to see that the markets did not crash this October as some thought it might! On the contrary, the markets were good world-wide. If you have a look at the good dates below (Trines etc) you will see how well the concept worked. The aspects made by the Sun to the outer planets after the Sun-Jupiter sextile of 8 October were mostly favorable, indicating a buying opportunity from the end of August, 2007 until possibly around the date of the Sun and Jupiter conjunction on December 23, 2007.

Take note that the Pluto moves into Capricorn at the end of January, 2008, which will bring pressure on corporations and governments and will probably be the start of a recession in the US and other countries. Investors should be very cautious, many astrologers agree that we are in for a hard landing.

Update January 2, 2008:

Right on cue, the markets started dropping in the new year, after the Sun-Jupiter conjunction a week ago. This is actually getting quite boring. I just want to talk about why I don't think that the markets will crash this year, around Monday, October 6, 2008, even though quite a few of the planetary conditions that cause crashes will be in effect at that time. Primarily, Saturn will be forming its opposition with Uranus: hard Uranus-Saturn aspects have definitely caused crashes and slumps in the past. The Sun will be square to Jupiter. Mercury will be turning retrograde on September 24th. But the reason I don't think it will crash that week is because of the benevolent aspects both Venus and Jupiter will be making to each other and the Sun and Saturn at the same time. This indicates that it is likely that there will be a big scare in the global stock markets around the first week of October, 2008, but that governments (Saturn/Jupiter) will inject massive amounts of money into the markets that will buoy them up for a while longer. Also, it is an even year. I think they will drop about 10 percent, and then recover again in preparation for the huge double-crashes of 2009 and

2011. That is why I still maintain that the first big crash will be around August 14, 2009.

(In hindsight: The markets dropped around 10 percent in the week leading up to October 6, 2008, the recorded date of the crash)

For those who think they can bottom-fish and pile back into the markets after the crash (like they did in mid-1988), please consider the possibility of a double-crash extending over the next few years, namely 2009 and again in 2011. Pension-fund managers, please be careful. The skies are turning black.

Update October 11, 2008:

I've been getting loads of emails from people who have lost half their money and are looking for some direction as to what they might consider doing.

I think it will rise in November for the next sextile, in fact, it could boom until mid next year, so I don't think you should accept defeat now and lock in your losses..... Unless you want to take an early gamble on gold, which I think is very undervalued at the moment in the light of the truly horrible T-square that is coming up in 2010 when I expect gold to be at least $2000-$3000 an ounce. The same planets were involved in a T-square similar to the one coming up at the start of World War 2. The only real difference is that it looks as if it will last slightly shorter than that period, this time possibly lasting about 4-5 years.

Saturn and Uranus will be in fortunate positions from about 2014-2017, especially 2016, which historically has indicated several boom periods, but looking ahead, I think that the first signs of recovery could start in about 2012, with maybe a few relatively small dips to go through before the next big rise in the global markets.

So, hang in, and hopefully this Uranus Saturn opposition (which is still closing in to the opposition at the end of this month) won't cause a full-blown crash like it did in October 1987 when they last conjunct.

Update October 13, 2008:

I spent some time these past few days thinking about what has happened under the current aspects, and am aware that many people might need some direction right now, other than the usual "if this happens, then do that, otherwise we will just have to wait and see" approach.

Exceptional times need exceptional measures. We have seen some classic examples of Saturn (governments, the status quo, fear, lack of confidence) in conflict with Uranus (sudden, unexpected and acerbic breakdowns, breakups) these past few weeks. The opposition of these two planets also had its expected effects on the world stock markets.

Many of you have lost a lot of money during this short period and are probably looking closely at the markets to try and cash in on the upswing when it occurs. I have decided that even though I am terrified myself in giving you a prediction that will cost you more money, this website deals primarily with gambling and that is what I will try and focus on right now.

These past few weeks, Mercury in its retrograde motion caused its usual havoc on discussions, communications, service delivery and transport. Mercury turns direct again on Wednesday, October 15. This will help tremendously in clearing the air in all the confusion surrounding these areas at this time. It is very likely that the G7 financial bailout agreement will work this time and in the short to medium term, the markets will react very favorably to this news, even though we are still under the influence of the two giant planets in opposition.

Therefore, this looks like an excellent time to start purchasing equities and the all-share stock indexes. The extent of a gamble you would like to take is up to you, but a good approach might be to put half of your available funds into the markets at this time, and the other half at the end of the month if things look like they are blasting off solidly.

From November onwards, the skies look fairly clear until mid-January 2009, when once again Saturn and Uranus come into conflict on the retrograde opposition. Note that this opposition has three passes, the 1987 crash only had the one, and hence the next year could be so much more volatile. On January 12, 2009, Mercury turns retrograde again, bringing its usual confusion to all kinds of communications. This is another possible time for chaos and breakdowns to occur, but because it is the retrograde pass, the outcome might be quite different. Jupiter conjoins the Sun around January 23rd. Often this has a lifting effect on the markets, but after following these aspects for a long time now I can report that this is the aspect that can cause this Sun-Jupiter theory to fail. It appears that this conjuction can go both ways, so please bear this in mind if you are following these aspects.

This potentially disruptive time lasts at least until the beginning of February when Mercury turns direct again. February 2009 might be another window of opportunity for investors looking for an upturn.

Update February 6, 2009:
As mentioned above, the markets rose approximately 20 percent worldwide from November last year until mid-January. From January 12, the exact day Mercury turned retrograde again, the world markets began to drop. The FTSE, for example, dropped for 13 straight sessions out of 14.

Update March 16, 2009:
This past week global markets have risen and investors are regaining confidence in the "rally in a bear market". Conditions look good for investing until early May 2009, when the Sun and Jupiter will form the next square aspect (see the "Square dates" below).

Update April 28, 2009:
On the page written in December 2006 on the left menu, Predictions for 2007-2008, I mentioned the possibility of a pandemic occurring towards 2009/2010 that could be caused by Uranus in its current position. I thought it would be avian flu, but it has turned out to be swine flu with some avian mutations. Being

viruses, both are ruled by the planet Uranus. People who do not understand planetary ruler ships must think I'm crazy, but that is how it works. Believe it or not, every possible thing under the sun is ruled by a planet, including viruses. It is interesting to note that as the Sun and Jupiter begin to square up, news has flooded across the world regarding the possibility of a swine flu pandemic. So, that appears to be the trigger for the global markets to plunge next week. If you are interested reading more about how I came to the conclusion that the planet Uranus is the likely ruler of viruses.

Update May 18, 2009:

Well, they didn't plunge last week and that's the last straw for me. All I can say is that if you follow these dates for a long time you will see that they are generally good indicators of the market movements, but there are sometimes exceptions like this one.

Final Update July 23, 2009:

Over the past few weeks, stock markets have boomed worldwide. There is a general feeling of optimism and investors are piling back into equities. Daily we are hearing stories of "green shoots", the bottom having been reached and that the recession is over. Exactly thirteen years ago I predicted and published a crash for next month. How do I feel now?

The markets came very close to crashing on the first Saturn-Uranus opposition ten months ago. They dropped again noticeably on the second pass in mid-January. In three weeks time, Saturn will once again move to within five degrees of opposing Uranus and be closing in. I do not think it is possible for the markets to break the pattern and withstand the effects. Elliott wave theorists have already noticed the massive head-and-shoulders pattern that has formed in the indices. I still think all mayhem is going to break loose towards the end of August. There will likely be violent uprisings and attacks flaring up around the world. Weak structures of all forms, physical and institutional, are going to once again be tested and collapse. I still think the global markets will crash severely. My only reservation is that it might happen a week or so after August 14, but very likely begin by the time Mercury turns retrograde on September 7, 2009. Let's just watch with interest.

My Apologies

I am embarrassed to say that this year both the Sun square Jupiter and Sun opposite Jupiter did not have the effects they usually do, even though the Chinese markets dropped 20% in August when they opposed. In 1996 I predicted that the markets would not be a good place to be in at the end of the 2000 decade, which proved to be true. In mitigation, although the crash date was out by ten months, the prediction was still over 93% accurate for a period of thirteen years ahead. In all fairness, perhaps pumping over a trillion dollars into the US economy alone changed things a little.

I was wrong about the crash date but am consoled that my prediction for the discovery of extra-terrestrial life, made unofficially in 2001 but archived on the net from 2005 onwards was accurate to within a few days.

What I've learned from this: The interaction of Saturn and Uranus, in particular, play a major role in affecting global equity conditions. Although I predicted a 10% drop when they first opposed in October 2008 (which was accompanied by the Sun squaring Jupiter in this case), I underestimated it by focusing too much on the second hit when they opposed in 2009 by looking too closely at the other planetary aspects at the time.

This page will no longer be updated. I still, however, have seen enough to believe that the planets do generally affect the markets and hope that the dates below can be of some use to you when making your decisions regarding timing and possible turning points in the future. I also believe that there will still be another crash before the end of 2011.

1.2. ABOUT THE INDUSTRY & OVERVIEW OF INDIAN MARKET

1.2.1 STOCK MARKET

Basically, Securities markets provide a channel for allocation of savings by an individual or an organization to those who have a productive need for them. So, a security market can be said a location where the savers meet the real investors who need the fund. The savers and investors are constrained by the economy's abilities to invest and save respectively which thus helps market in enhancing savings and investment in the economy. Stock Market is therefore affected by the dynamics of the economic, political, cultural and environmental activities within the country and rest of the world.

The securities markets in India have witnessed several policy initiatives, which has refined the market micro-structure, modernized operations and broadened investment choices for the investors.

Indian Share Market is the oldest Asian stock market incorporated in 1875. The name of the first share trading association in India was Native Share and Stock Broker's Association which later came to be known as Bombay Stock Exchange. This association started with 318 members.

The National Stock Exchange (NSE) is India's latest exchange which commenced from June 30, 1994. The main objectives of the NSE are to provide speedy transactions, fast settlements and to benefit the small investors who find it difficult to sell shares at BSE.

The past decade has been quite remarkable for the Securities market in India with the boom in the economy fueled by better banking system. It has grown exponentially and the market has also witnessed fundamental institutional changes. There have also been significant improvements in efficiency, transparency and safety.

1.2.2 NSE

The National Stock Exchange of India Limited has genesis in the report of the High Powered Study Group on Establishment of New Stock Exchanges. It recommended promotion of a National Stock Exchange by financial institutions (FIs) to provide access to investors from all across the country on an equal footing. Based on the recommendations, NSE was promoted by leading Financial Institutions at the behest of the Government of India and was incorporated in November 1992 as a tax-paying company unlike other stock exchanges in the country.

The National Stock Exchange (NSE) operates a nation-wide, electronic market, offering trading in Capital Market, Derivatives Market and Currency Derivatives segments including equities, equities based derivatives, Currency futures and options, equity based ETFs, Gold ETF and Retail Government Securities. Today NSE network stretches to more than 1,500 locations in the country and supports more than 2, 30,000 terminals.

With more than 10 asset classes in offering, NSE has taken many initiatives to strengthen the securities industry and provides several new products like Mini Nifty, Long Dated Options and Mutual Fund Service System. Responding to market needs, NSE has introduced services like DMA, FIX capabilities, co-location facility and mobile trading to cater to the evolving need of the market and various categories of market participants.

NSE has made its global presence felt with cross-listing arrangements, including license agreements covering benchmark indexes for U.S. and Indian equities with CME Group and has also signed a Memorandum of Understanding (MOU) with Singapore Exchange (SGX) to cooperate in the development of a market for India-linked products and services to be listed on SGX. The two exchanges also will look into a bilateral securities trading link to enable investors in one country to seamlessly trade on the other country's exchange.

NSE is committed to operate a market ecosystem which is transparent and at the same time offers high levels of safety, integrity and corporate governance, providing ever growing trading & investment opportunities for investors.

NSE provides exposure to investors in two types of markets, namely:

A) Wholesale debt market

B) Capital market

A) WHOLESALE DEBT MARKET

Similar to money market operations, debt market operations involve institutional investors and corporate bodies entering into transactions of high value in financial instruments like treasury bills, government securities, etc.

Trading at NSE

• Fully automated screen-based trading mechanism

• Strictly follows the principle of an order-driven market

• Trading members are linked through a communication network

• This network allows them to execute trade from their offices

• The prices at which the buyer and seller are willing to transact will appear on the screen.

• When the prices match the transaction will be completed , a confirmation slip will be printed at the office of the trading member.

Advantages of trading at NSE

• Integrated network for trading in stock market of India

• Fully automated screen based system that provides higher degree of transparency

• Investors can transact from any part of the country at uniform prices

• Greater functional efficiency supported by totally computerized network

B)   CAPITAL MARKET

S&P CNX DEFTY

Almost every institutional investor and off-shore fund enterprise with an equity exposure in India would like to have an instrument for measuring returns on their equity investment in dollar terms. To facilitate this, a new index the S&P CNX Defty-Dollar Denominated S&P CNX Nifty has been developed. S&P CNX Defty is S&P CNX Nifty, measured in dollars.

Salient Features

- Performance indicator to foreign institutional investors, off-shore funds, etc.
- Provides an effective tool for hedging Indian equity exposure.
- Impact cost of the S&P CNX Nifty for a portfolio size of Rs.50 Lakhs is 0.06%
- Provides fund managers an instrument for measuring returns on their equity investment in dollar terms.

Calculation of S&P CNX Defty

Computations are done using the S&P CNX Nifty index calculated on the NEAT trading system of NSE and INR-USD exchange rate that is based on the real time polled data feed.

$$S\&P\ CNX\ Defty = \frac{S\&P\ CNX\ Nifty\ at\ time\ t\ *\ Exchange\ rate\ as\ on\ base\ date}{Exchange\ rate\ at\ time\ t}$$

Calculation of closing value of S&P CNX Defty

Closing value of S&P CNX Defty is computed by considering average of INR-USD polled data values (exchange rate) of last 30 minutes of the market.

$$\textbf{Closing value of S\&P CNX Defty} = \frac{Closing\ value\ of\ S\&P\ CNX\ Nifty\ *\ Exchange\ rate\ as\ on\ base\ date}{Average\ of\ exchange\ rate\ of\ last\ 30\ minutes\ of\ the\ market.}$$

1.2.3 FII

When a group of investors or an institution invests there funds in the financial market of a foreign company. Institutional investors includes Pension Funds, Mutual Funds, Investment Trust, Insurance or reinsurance companies, Endowment Funds, University Funds, Banks, Hedge Funds, Asset Management Funds etc.

Countries like India attract FII's because of their robust domestic growth, fast growing economy, skilled labour and cost competitiveness. The term FII is used commonly in India to refer to outside companies investing in the financial market of India. In order to trade in Indian equity market international institutional investors must register themselves with the (SEBI) Securities and Exchange Board of India to participate in the market as SEBI have prescribed norms to register FIIs and also to regulate such investments flowing in through FIIs

The eligibility criteria for applicant seeking fii registration as per regulation 6 of SEBI (FII) regulations, 1995, foreign institutional investors are required to fulfill the following conditions to qualify for grant of registration:

• Applicant should have track record, professional competence, financial soundness, experience, general reputation of fairness and integrity.

• The applicant should be regulated by an appropriate foreign regulatory authority in the same capacity/category where registration is sought from SEBI. Registration with authorities, which are responsible for incorporation, is not adequate to qualify as Foreign Institutional Investor.

• The applicant is required to have the permission under the provisions of the Foreign Exchange Management Act, 1999 from the Reserve Bank of India.

• Applicant must be legally permitted to invest in securities outside the country or its in-corporation / establishment.

• The applicant must be a "fit and proper" person.

• The applicant has to appoint a local custodian and enter into an agreement with the custodian. Besides it also has to appoint a designated bank to route its transactions.

• Payment of registration fee of US $ 5,000.00 "Form A" as prescribed in SEBI (FII) Regulations, 1995 is to be filled before applying for FII registration.

SUPPORTING DOCUMENTS REQUIRED ARE:

• Application in Form A duly signed by the authorized signatory of the applicant.

• Certified copy of the relevant clauses or articles of the Memorandum and Articles of Association or the agreement authorizing the applicant to invest on behalf of its clients.

• Audited financial statements and annual reports for the last one year, provided that the period covered shall not be less than twelve months.

• A declaration by the applicant with registration number and other particulars in support of its registration or regulation by a Securities Commission or Self Regulatory Organisation or any other appropriate regulatory authority with whom the applicant is registered in its home country.

• A declaration by the applicant that it has entered into a custodian agreement with a domestic custodian together with particulars of the domestic custodian.

• A signed declaration statement that appears at the end of the Form.

•Declaration regarding fit & proper entity. The fee for registration as FII is US $ 5,000. The mode of payment is Demand Draft in favour of "Securities and Exchange Board of India" payable at New York".

Agencies Regulating FII in India

- RBI : The apex bank
- FIPB : Review all foreign investment proposals
- SEBI : Regulates India's capital market

Advantages of FII

- Increases Forex reserves
- Increases domestic savings
- Increases domestic investments
- Availability of capital reserve

Disadvantages of FII

- Problem of inflation
- False representation of economy
- Problem for small investors
- Hot Money

FII investment is frequently referred to as hot money for the reason that it can leave the country at the same speed at which it comes in.

EXCHANGE CONTROLS

FIIs are required to open up one or more bank accounts with certain designated banks and must also appoint a domestic custodian for custody of investment made by the FII. Through the designated accounts, FIIs are authorized to freely transfer funds from foreign currency accounts to Rupee accounts and vice versa; make Rupee denominated investments in Indian companies; freely transfer after-tax proceeds from Rupee accounts to foreign currency accounts, and repatriate capital, capital gain, dividends interest income and other gains, subject to deduction for applicable withholding taxes. So long as FIIs execute purchases and sales on a recognized Indian stock exchange, they are not required to obtain transaction specific approval from the Reserve Bank. FIIs are also entitled to effect transactions using their own proprietary funds, or the funds of their sub accounts.

1.2.3.1 Current scenario

India is the most popular destination for overseas portfolio investors to park their fund in the Asian region for 2010. It may be a signal of increasing confidence in the Indian growth story, when the rest of the world is struggling to fight the recession.

Foreign investors have turned optimistic on the Indian market and invested a whopping Rs 5,200 crore (about USD 1.16 billion) so far this month in contrast to heavy outflows witnessed in February.

Till March 16, foreign institutional investors (FIIs) have invested Rs 5,232.70 crore (Rs 52.32 billion) in equities and bonds, taking total net inflows in 2011 so far to Rs 7,326.70 crore (Rs 73.26 billion), as per the data available with the Securities and Exchange Board of India(SEBI).

In February, FIIs pulled out a net Rs 3,269.80 crore (Rs 32.69 billion) from the domestic market. In dollar terms, net FII outflows stood at $ 721.33 million.

According to analysts, FII flows gushed after getting positive cues from the 2011-12 Budgets. However, at global level, uncertainty prevails on account of factors like the crisis in Middle East and North Africa region (MENA).

Hardening of global commodity prices along with high crude prices are, deterring foreign investors from putting money into emerging markets.

Overseas investors have been gross buyers of equities worth Rs 2,354.10 crore (Rs 23.54 billion) so far this month and infused Rs 2,878.60 crore (Rs 28.78 billion) in the debt market, taking their net investment during the month to Rs 5,232.70 crore (Rs 52.32 billion).

While indicating that positive impact of the Budget 2011-12 is responsible for resurgent foreign inflows, market analysts further predict that foreign fund houses will keep investing in Indian bourses in the coming days too.

"The FII inflows in March have been strong. This may be because of the better-than-expected Budget," said SMC Capitals Head of Research, Jagannathan Thunuguntla.

In January, overseas investors were gross buyers of equities worth Rs 79,420 crore (Rs 794.20 billion), but sold shares worth Rs 72,910 crore (Rs 729.10 billion), translating into a net investment of Rs 6,509.60 crore (Rs 65.09 billion), as per the SEBI data.

FIIs have been the gross sellers of equities worth Rs 7,044.40 crore (Rs 70.44 billion) in 2011 so far, but they were bullish on the debt market, with an investment of Rs 14,371.10 crore (Rs 143.71 billion), taking the net investment to Rs 7,326.70 crore (Rs 73.26 billion).

In dollar terms, net FII inflows amount to about $ 1.63 billion in 2011 so far. In 2010, foreign investors bought stocks and bonds valued at nearly Rs 10 lakh crore, a record number in a year.

At the same time, FIIs sold shares and bonds worth Rs 7.8 lakh crore during the year - which implied a record net investment of over Rs 1.75 lakh crore for the year. In dollar terms, net FII inflows stood at about $ 39 billion in 2010.

1.2.4 FOREIGN EXCHANGE MARKET

1.2.4.1 INTRODUCTION

Foreign exchange (forex or FX for short) is one of the most exciting, fast-paced markets around. Until recently, trading in the forex market had been the domain of large financial institutions, corporations, central banks, hedge funds and extremely wealthy individuals. The emergence of the internet has changed all of this, and now it is possible for average investors to buy and sell currencies easily with the click of a mouse.

1.2.4.2 WHAT IS IT?

The foreign exchange market is the "place" where currencies are traded. Currencies are important to most people around the world, whether they realize it or not, because currencies need to be exchanged in order to conduct foreign trade and business. If you are living in the U.S. and want to buy cheese from France, either you or the company that you buy the cheese from has to pay the French for the cheese in Euros (EUR). This means that the U.S. importer would have to exchange the equivalent value of U.S. dollars (USD) into Euros. The same goes for travelling. A French tourist in Egypt can't pay in Euros to see the pyramids because it's not the locally accepted currency. As such, the tourist has to exchange the euros for the local currency, in this case the Egyptian pound, at the current exchange rate.

One unique aspect of this international market is that there is no central marketplace for currency exchange. Rather, trade is conducted electronically over-the-counter (OTC), which means that all transactions occur via computer networks between traders around the world, rather than on one centralized exchange. The market is open 24 hours a day, five and a half days a week, and currencies are traded worldwide in the major financial centres of London, New York, Tokyo, Zurich, Frankfurt, Hong Kong, Singapore, Paris and Sydney - across almost every time zone. This means that when the trading day in the U.S. ends, the forex market begins anew in Tokyo and Hong Kong. As such, the forex market can be extremely active any time of the day, with price quotes changing constantly.

1.2.4.3 SPOT MARKET AND THE FORWARDS AND FUTURES MARKETS

There are actually three ways that institutions, corporations and individuals trade

Forex

The spot market, the forwards market and the futures market. The spot market always has been the largest market because it is the "underlying" real asset that the forwards and futures markets are based on. In the past, the futures market was the most popular venue for traders because it was available to individual investors for a longer period of time. However, with the advent of electronic trading, the spot market has witnessed a huge surge in activity and now surpasses the futures market as the preferred trading market for individual investors and speculators. When people refer to the forex market, they usually are referring to the spot market. The forwards and futures markets tend to be more popular with companies that need to hedge their foreign exchange risks out to a specific date in the future.

Spot Market

More specifically, the spot market is where currencies are bought and sold according to the current price. That price, determined by supply and demand, is a reflection of many things, including current interest rates, economic performance, sentiment towards ongoing political situations (both locally and internationally), as well as the perception of the future performance of one currency against another. When a deal is finalized, this is known as a "spot deal". It is a bilateral transaction by which one party delivers an agreed-upon currency amount to the counter party and receives a specified amount of another currency at the agreed-upon exchange rate value. After a position is closed, the settlement is in cash. Although the spot market is commonly known as one that deals with transactions in the present (rather than the future), these trades actually take two days for settlement.

Forwards and Futures Markets

Unlike the spot market, the forwards and futures markets do not trade actual currencies. Instead they deal in contracts that represent claims to a certain currency type, a specific price per unit and a future date for settlement. In the forwards market, contracts are bought and sold OTC between two parties, who determine the terms of the agreement between themselves.

In the futures market, future contracts are bought and sold based upon a standard size and settlement date on public commodities markets, such as the Chicago Mercantile Exchange. In the U.S., the National Futures Association regulates the futures market. Futures contracts have specific details, including the number of units being traded, delivery and settlement dates, and minimum price increments that cannot be customized. The exchange acts as a counterpart to the trader, providing clearance and settlement.

Both types of contracts are binding and are typically settled for cash for the exchange in question upon expiry, although contracts can also be bought and sold before they expire. The forwards and futures markets can offer protection against risk when trading currencies. Usually, big international corporations use these markets in order to hedge against future exchange rate fluctuations, but speculators take part in these markets as well.

1.2.4.4 READING A QUOTE AND UNDERSTANDING THE JARGON

One of the biggest sources of confusion for those new to the currency market is the standard for quoting currencies.

Reading a Quote

When a currency is quoted, it is done in relation to another currency, so that the value of one is reflected through the value of another. Therefore, if you are trying to determine the exchange rate between the U.S. dollar (USD) and the Japanese yen (JPY), the quote would look like this:

USD/INR = 50.53

This is referred to as a currency pair. The currency to the left of the slash is the base currency, while the currency on the right is called the quote or counter currency. The base currency (in this case, the U.S. dollar) is always equal to one unit (in this case, US$1), and the quoted currency (in this case, the Indian Rs.) is what that one base unit is equivalent to in the other currency. The quote means that US$1 = 50.53 Indian Rs. In other words, US$1 can buy 50.53 Indian Rs.

Direct Quote vs. Indirect Quote

There are two ways to quote a currency pair, either directly or indirectly. A direct quote is simply a currency pair in which the domestic currency is the base currency; while an indirect quote, is a currency pair where the domestic currency is the quoted currency. So if you were looking at the Canadian dollar as the domestic currency and U.S. dollar as the foreign currency, a direct quote would be CAD/USD, while an indirect quote would be USD/CAD. The direct quote varies the foreign currency, and the quoted, or domestic currency, remains fixed at one unit. In the indirect quote, on the other hand, the domestic currency is variable and the foreign currency is fixed at one unit.

For example, if Canada is the domestic currency, a direct quote would be 0.85 CAD/USD, which means with C$1, you can purchase US$0.85. The indirect quote for this would be the inverse (1/0.85), which is 1.18 USD/CAD and means that USD$1 will purchase C$1.18.

Cross Currency

When a currency quote is given without the U.S. dollar as one of its components, this is called a cross currency. The most common cross currency pairs are the USD/INR, EUR/GBP, EUR/CHF and EUR/JPY.

Bid and Ask

As with most trading in the financial markets, when you are trading a currency pair there is a (buy) and an (sell). Again, these are in relation to the base currency. When buying a currency pair (going bid price ask price long), the ask price refers to the amount of quoted currency that has to be paid in order to buy one unit of the base currency, or how much the market will sell one unit of the base currency for in relation to the quoted currency. The bid price is used when selling a currency pair (going short) and reflects how much of the quoted currency will be obtained when selling one unit of the base currency, or how much the market will pay for the quoted currency in relation to the base currency. The quote before the slash is the bid price, and the two digits after the slash represent the ask price (only the last two digits of the full price are typically quoted). Note that the bid price is always smaller than the ask price. Let's look at an example:

USD/CAD = 1.2000/05 Bid = 1.2000 Ask= 1.2005

Spreads and Pips

The difference between the bid price and the ask price is called a spread. If we were to look at the following quote: EUR/USD = 1.2500/03, the spread would be 0.0003 or 3 pips, also known as points. Although these movements may seem insignificant, even the smallest point change can result in thousands of dollars being made or lost due to leverage. Again, this is one of the reasons that speculators are so attracted to the forex market; even the tiniest price movement can result in huge profit.

Currency Pairs in the Forwards and Futures Markets

One of the key technical differences between the forex markets is the way currencies are quoted. In the forwards or futures markets, foreign exchange always is quoted against the U.S. dollar. This means that pricing is done in terms of how many U.S. dollars are needed to buy one unit of the other currency. Remember that in the spot market some currencies are quoted against the U.S. dollar, while for others, the U.S. dollar is being quoted against them. As such, the forwards/futures market and the spot market quotes will not always be parallel one another.

For example, in the spot market, the British pound is quoted against the U.S. dollar as GBP/USD. This is the same way it would be quoted in the forwards and futures markets. Thus, when the British pound strengthens against the U.S. dollar in the spot market, it will also rise in the forwards and futures markets.

On the other hand, when looking at the exchange rate for the U.S. dollar and the Japanese yen, the former is quoted against the latter. In the spot market, the quote would be 115 for example, which means that one U.S. dollar would buy 115 Japanese yen. In the futures market, it would be quoted as (1/115) or .0087, which means that 1 Japanese yen would buy .0087 U.S. dollars. As such, a rise in the USD/JPY spot rate would equate to a decline in the JPY futures rate because the U.S. dollar would have strengthened against the Japanese yen and therefore one Japanese yen would buy less U.S. dollars.

1.2.4.5 Differences between Forex and Equities

A major difference between the forex and equities markets is the number of traded instruments: the forex market has very few compared to the thousands found in the equities market. The majority of forex traders focus their efforts on seven different currency pairs: the four majors, which include (EUR/USD, USD/JPY, GBP/USD, USD/CHF); and the three commodity pairs (USD/CAD, AUD/USD, NZD/USD). All other pairs are just different combinations of the same currencies, otherwise known as cross currencies. This makes currency trading easier to follow because rather than having to cherry-pick between 10,000 stocks to find the best value, all that FX traders need to do is "keep up" on the economic and political news of eight countries.

Due to the extreme liquidity of the forex market, margins are low and leverage is high. It just is not possible to find such low margin rates in the equities markets; most margin traders in the equities markets need at least 50% of the value of the investment available as margin, whereas forex traders need as little as 1%. Furthermore, commissions in the equities market are much higher than in the forex market. Traditional brokers ask for commission fees on top of the spread, plus the fees that have to be paid to the exchange. Spot forex brokers take only the spread as their fee for the transaction.

1.2.4.6 THE HISTORY OF THE FOREX

Gold Standard System

The creation of the gold standard monetary system in 1875 marks one of the most important events in the history of the forex market. Before the gold standard was implemented, countries would commonly use gold and silver as means of international payment. The main issue with using gold and silver for payment is that their value is affected by external supply and demand. For example, the discovery of a new gold mine would drive gold prices down.

The underlying idea behind the gold standard was that governments guaranteed the conversion of currency into a specific amount of gold, and vice versa. In other words, a currency would be backed by gold. Obviously, governments needed a fairly substantial gold reserve in order to meet the demand for exchanges. During the late nineteenth century, all of the major economic countries had defined an amount of currency to an ounce of gold. Over time, the difference in price of an ounce of gold between two currencies became the exchange rate for those two currencies. This represented the first standardized means of currency exchange in history.

The gold standard eventually broke down during the beginning of World War I. Due to the political tension with Germany, the major European powers felt a need to complete large military projects. The financial burden of these projects was so substantial that there was not enough gold at the time to exchange for all the excess currency that the governments were printing off.

Although the gold standard would make a small comeback during the inter-war years, most countries had dropped it again by the onset of World War II. However, gold never ceased being the ultimate form of monetary value.

Bretton Woods System

Before the end of World War II, the Allied nations believed that there would be a need to set up a monetary system in order to fill the void that was left behind when the gold standard system was abandoned. In July 1944, more than 700 representatives from the Allies convened at Bretton Woods, New Hampshire, to deliberate over what would be called the Bretton Woods system of international monetary management.

To simplify, Bretton Woods led to the formation of the following:

1. A method of fixed exchange rates;

2. The U.S. dollar replacing the gold standard to become a primary reserve currency; and

3. The creation of three international agencies to oversee economic activity: the International Monetary Fund (IMF), International Bank for Reconstruction and Development, and the General Agreement on Tariffs and Trade (GATT).

One of the main features of Bretton Woods is that the U.S. dollar replaced gold as the main standard of convertibility for the world's currencies; and furthermore, the U.S. dollar became the only currency that would be backed by gold. (This turned out to be the primary reason that Bretton Woods eventually failed.)

Over the next 25 or so years, the U.S. had to run a series of balance of payment deficits in order to be the world's reserved currency. By the early 1970s, U.S. gold reserves were so depleted that the U.S. treasury did not have enough gold to cover all the U.S. dollars that foreign central banks had in reserve.

Finally, on August 15, 1971, U.S. President Richard Nixon closed the gold window, and the U.S. announced to the world that it would no longer exchange gold for the U.S. dollars that were held in foreign reserves. This event marked the end of Bretton Woods.

Even though Bretton Woods didn't last, it left an important legacy that still has a significant effect on today's international economic climate. This legacy exists in the form of the three international agencies created in the 1940s: the IMF, the International Bank for Reconstruction and Development (now part of the World Bank) and GATT, the precursor to the World Trade Organization.

1.2.4.7 Current Exchange System

After the Bretton Woods system broke down, the world finally accepted the use of floating foreign exchange rates during the Jamaica agreement of 1976. This meant that the use of the gold standard would be permanently abolished. However, this is not to say that governments adopted a pure free-floating exchange rate system. Most governments employ one of the following three exchange rate systems that are still used today:

1. Dollarization;

2. Pegged rate; and

3. Managed floating rate.

Dollarization

This event occurs when a country decides not to issue its own currency and adopts a foreign currency as its national currency. Although dollarization usually enables a country to be seen as a more stable place for investment, the drawback is that the country's central bank can no longer print money or make any sort of monetary policy. An example of dollarization is El Salvador's use of the U.S. dollar.

Pegged Rates

Pegging occurs when one country directly fixes its exchange rate to a foreign currency so that the country will have somewhat more stability than a normal float. More specifically, pegging allows a country's currency to be exchanged at a fixed rate with a single or a specific basket of foreign currencies. The currency will only fluctuate when the pegged currencies change.

For example, China pegged its yuan to the U.S. dollar at a rate of 8.28 yuan to US$1, between 1997 and July 21, 2005. The downside to pegging would be that a currency's value is at the mercy of the pegged currency's economic situation. For example, if the U.S. dollar appreciates substantially against all other currencies, the yuan would also appreciate, which may not be what the Chinese central bank wants.

Managed Floating Rates

This type of system is created when a currency's exchange rate is allowed to freely change in value subject to the market forces of supply and demand. However, the government or central bank may intervene to stabilize extreme fluctuations in exchange rates. For example, if a country's currency is depreciating far beyond an acceptable level, the government can raise short-term interest rates. Raising rates should cause the currency to appreciate slightly; but understand that this is a very simplified example. Central banks typically employ a number of tools to manage currency.

1.2.4.8 FACTORS INFLUENCING FOREIGN EXCHANGE RATE

There are several factors which affect and decide the exchange rate of currencies, causing frequent fluctuations in the rate. Sometimes the exchange rate may change over a period of some months or years and sometimes fluctuations occur within a span of some hours and days. Theoretically, in a free market, the rate of exchange is determined by the demand for and supply of foreign currency. The equilibrium rate of exchange is attained at the point where demand for foreign currency is exactly equal to its supply. The demand and supply of foreign currency arise from international trade, investments and other international transactions. For example- If India imports some goods from the U.S. India will require US dollars to pay for those imports. This is demand for dollars and supply of Rupees in exchange, in the foreign exchange, market. India will buy dollars, against Rupees to pay for its imports. Whereas, if India exports some goods or services to the US, there will be a demand for Indian Rupees by the US to pay for its imports from India. This is basic economics, that demand and supply keep adjusting till they become equal and the equilibrium rate is achieved. But this ideal equilibrium rate is difficult to achieve because demand and supply are affected by several factors, which cause frequent fluctuations and adjustments in the exchange rate, fixing it at a rate which may not be the equilibrium rate.

INTERNATIONAL TRADE

Trade of goods and services between countries is the major reason for the demand and supply of foreign currencies. The value or strength or weakness of a countries currency in terms of other currencies depends on its trade with those countries. If a country's imports are higher, the demand for foreign currency in this country will be high. Higher demand for foreign currency means high value of foreign currency and low value of the domestic currency. This is a typical case for underdeveloped countries which rely on imports for development needs. The current account balance (deficit or surplus) thus reflects the strength and weakness of the domestic currency.

CAPITAL MOVEMENTS

International investments in the form of Foreign direct investment (FDI) and Foreign institutional investments (FII) have become the most important factors affecting the exchange rate in today's open world economy. Countries which attract large capital inflows through foreign investments, will witness an appreciation in its domestic currency as its demand rises. Outflow of capital would mean a depreciation of domestic currency.

CHANGE IN PRICES

Domestic inflation or deflation affects the exchange rate by affecting the demand and supply of domestic currency in the foreign exchange market. For example, if prices in India go up, making Indian goods costlier, the demand for Indian goods will do down. When exports go down, the demand for rupee will fall, causing depreciation in its exchange value.

SPECULATIONS

Uncertainties are always there in the financial market. Speculators predict about the future exchange rate based on various happenings in the world, in various countries. Speculators study the various ups and downs of a country and its resilience to international happenings and forecast the possible future exchange rate based on a particular countries economic strengths and weaknesses. If the speculators expect a fall in the value of a currency, in the near future, they will sell that currency and start buying the other currency that they expect to appreciate. The selling of the former currency will thus increase its supply in the foreign exchange market and bring down its value. The other currency appreciates as its demand increases.

STRENGTH OF THE ECONOMY

If the economic fundamentals of a country are strong, the exchange rate of its domestic currency remains stable and strong. Fiscal balance, international current account balance, international liabilities, foreign exchange reserves, resilience to international trade fluctuations, GDP, inflation rate all are indicators of a country's economic strength.

GOVERNMENT POLICIES

In countries where there is fixed or managed float, the central bank becomes an important player in the foreign exchange market. The bank influences the value of the currency by its market operations like buying and selling of bills and currencies. The bank rate also influences the exchange rate by influencing investments and thereby the demand and supply of the domestic currency.

STOCK EXCHANGE OPERATIONS

Stock exchange operations in foreign securities, debenture, stocks and shares, influence the demand and supply of related currencies, thus influencing their exchange rate.

POLITICAL FACTORS

Political scenario of the country ultimately decides the strength of the country. Stable efficient government at the centre will encourage positive development in the country, creating investor confidence and a good image in the international market. An economy with a strong, positive image will obviously have a strong domestic currency. This is the reason why speculations rise considerably during the parliament elections, with various predictions, of the future government and its policies. In 1998, the Indian rupee depreciated against the dollar due to the American sanctions after India conducted the Pokharan nuclear test. Value of a currency is thus not a simple result of its demand and supply, but a complex mix of multiple factors influencing the demand and supply. It's a tight rope walk for any country to maintain a strong, stable currency, with policies taking care of conflicting demands like inflation and export promotion, welcoming foreign investments and avoiding an appreciation of the domestic currency, all at the same time.

ECONOMIC DATA

Economic theories may move currencies in the long term, but on a shorter-term, day-to-day or week-to-week basis, economic data has a more significant impact. It is often said the biggest companies in the world are actually countries and that their currency is essentially shares in that country. Economic data, such as the latest gross domestic product (GDP) numbers, are often considered to be like a company's latest earnings data. In the same way that financial news and current events can affect a company's stock price, news and information about a country can have a major impact on the direction of that country's currency. Changes in interest rates, inflation, unemployment, consumer confidence, GDP, political stability etc. can all lead to extremely large gains/losses depending on the nature of the announcement and the current state of the country.

The number of economic announcements made each day from around the world can be intimidating, but as one spends more time learning about the forex market it becomes clear which announcements have the greatest influence. Listed below are a number of economic indicators that are generally considered to have the greatest influence - regardless of which country the announcement comes from.

Employment Data

Most countries release data about the number of people that currently are employed within that economy. In the U.S., this data is known as non-farm payrolls and is released the first Friday of the month by the Bureau of Labor Statistics. In most cases, strong increases in employment signal that a country enjoys a prosperous economy, while decreases are a sign of potential contraction. If a country has gone recently through economic troubles, strong employment data could send the currency higher because it is a sign of economic health and recovery. On the other hand, high employment can also lead to inflation, so this data could send the currency downward. In other words, economic data and the movement of currency will often depend on the circumstances that exist when the data is released.

Interest Rates

As was seen with some of the economic theories, interest rates are a major focus in the forex market. The most focus by market participants, in terms of interest rates, is placed on the country's central bank changes of its bank rate, which is used to adjust monetary supply and institute the country's monetary policy. In the U.S., the Federal Open Market Committee (FOMC) determines the bank rate, or the rate at which commercial banks can borrow and lend to the U.S. Treasury.

The FOMC meets eight times a year to make decisions on whether to raise, lower or leave the bank rate the same; and each meeting, along with the minutes, is a point of focus.

Inflation

Inflation data measures the increases and decreases of price levels over a period of time. Due to the sheer amount of goods and services within an economy, a basket of goods and services is used to measure changes in prices. Price increases are a sign of inflation, which suggests that the country will see its currency depreciate. In the U.S., inflation data is shown in the Consumer Price Index, which is released on a monthly basis by the Bureau of Labor Statistics.

Gross Domestic Product

The gross domestic product of a country is a measure of all of the finished goods and services that a country generated during a given period. The GDP calculation is split into four categories: private consumption, government spending, business spending and total net exports. GDP is considered the best overall measure of the health of a country's economy, with GDP increases signaling economic growth. The healthier a country's economy is, the more attractive it is to foreign investors, which in turn can often lead to increases in the value of its currency, as money moves into the country. In the U.S., this data is released by the Bureau of Economic Analysis once a month in the third or fourth quarter of the month. *Retail Sales* Retail sales data measures the amount of sales that retailers make during the period, reflecting consumer spending. The measure itself doesn't look at all stores, but, similar to GDP, uses a group of stores of varying types to get an idea of consumer spending. This measure also gives market participants an idea of the strength of the economy, where increased spending signals a strong economy. In the U.S., the Department of Commerce releases data on retail sales around the middle of the month.

Durable Goods

The data for durable goods (those with a lifespan of more than three years) measures the amount of manufactured goods that are ordered, shipped and unfilled for the time period. These goods include such things as cars and appliances, giving economists an idea of the amount of individual spending on these longer-term goods, along with an idea of the health of the factory sector. This measure again gives market participants insight into the health of the economy, with data being released around the 26th of the month by the Department of Commerce.

Trade and Capital

Flows Interactions between countries create huge monetary flows that can have a substantial impact on the value of currencies. As was mentioned before, a country that imports far more than it exports could see its currency decline due to its need to sell its own currency to purchase the currency of the exporting nation. Furthermore, increased investments in a country can lead to substantial increases in the value of its currency.

Trade flow data looks at the difference between a country's imports and exports, with a trade deficit occurring when imports are greater than exports. In the U.S., the Commerce Department releases balance of trade data on a monthly basis, which shows the amount of goods and services that the U.S. exported and imported during the past month. Capital flow data looks at the difference in the amount of currency being brought in through investment and/or exports to currency being sold for foreign investments and/or imports. A country that is seeing a lot of foreign investment, where outsiders are purchasing domestic assets such as stocks or real estate, will generally have a capital flow surplus.

Balance of payments data is the combined total of a country's trade and capital flow over a period of time. The balance of payments is split into three categories: the current account, the capital account and the financial account. The current account looks at the flow of goods and services between countries. The capital account looks at the exchange of money between countries for the purpose of purchasing capital assets. The financial account looks at the monetary flow between countries for investment purposes.

Macroeconomic and Geopolitical

Events The biggest changes in the forex often come from macroeconomic and geopolitical events such as wars, elections, monetary policy changes and financial crises. These events have the ability to change or reshape the country, including its fundamentals. For example, wars can put a huge economic strain on a country and greatly increase the volatility in a region, which could impact the value of its currency. It is important to keep up to date on these macroeconomic and geopolitical events.

There is so much data that is released in the forex market that it can be very difficult for the average individual to know which data to follow. Despite this, it is important to know what news releases will affect the currencies you trade.

1.2.4.9 BALANCE OF PAYMENTS THEORY

A country's balance of payments is comprised of two segments - the current account and the capital account - which measure the inflows and outflows of goods and capital for a country. The balance of payments theory looks at the current account, which is the account dealing with trade of tangible goods, to get an idea of exchange-rate directions.

If a country is running a large current account surplus or deficit, it is a sign that a country's exchange rate is out of equilibrium. To bring the current account back into equilibrium, the exchange rate will need to adjust over time. If a country is running a large deficit (more imports than exports), the domestic currency will depreciate. On the other hand, a surplus would lead to currency appreciation. The balance of payments identity is found by:

$$BCA + BKA + BRA = 0$$

Where BCA represents the current account balance; BKA represents the capital account balance; and BRA represents the reserves account balance.

PART – 2 PRIMARY STUDIES

2.1 INTRODUCTION OF RESEARCH AREA

Finance is the buzz word all around the world. It is the one which makes the business go around and all aspects of the economy start and end at it. In today's competitive world the easiest way to accumulate wealth for new upcoming and promising ventures is to go public or turn towards masses through stock markets where small savings of these people can make miracles by investing wisely in reliable businesses and help managements of these companies to make them biggest companies in the world. Today many Indian companies are running their businesses in international market and these transactions may get affected by foreign exchange rate.

2.2 LITERATURE REVIEW

BAHMANI-OSKOOEE, MOHSEN & SOHRABIAN, AHMAD (1992) Shows relation between stock prices and exchange rates is very poor and includes few studies that have argued that exchange rate changes do affect stock prices. By relying on the portfolio approach to exchange rate determination, it is argued that a change in stock prices could also have an impact on exchange rates, i.e. there could be a two-way relationship between exchange rates and stock prices. Granger concept of causality as well as co integration technique are employed to support this conjecture. The empirical results show that there is bidirectional causality between stock prices measured by S&P 500 index and the effective exchange rate of the dollar, at least in the short-run. The co integration analysis reveals that there is no long-run relationship between two variables.

AJAYI, RICHARD A & MOUGOUÉ, MBODJA (1996) examines the intertemporal relation between stock indices and exchange rates for a sample of eight advanced economies. An error correction model (ECM) of the two variables is employed to simultaneously estimate the short-run and long-run dynamics of the variables. The ECM results reveal significant short-run and long-run feedback relations between the two financial markets. Specifically, the results show that an increase in aggregate domestic stock price has a negative short-run effect on domestic currency value. In the long run, however, increases in stock prices have a positive effect on domestic currency value. On the other hand, currency depreciation has a negative short-run and long-run effect on the stock market.

ABDALLA, ISSAM S.A & MURINDE, VICTOR (1997) investigated relationship between exchange rates and stock prices in the emerging financial markets of India, Korea, Pakistan and the Philippines. The motivation is to establish the causal linkages between leading prices in the foreign exchange market and the stock market; the linkages have implications for the ongoing attempts to develop stock markets in emerging economies simultaneously with a policy shift towards independently floating exchange rates. Some recent econometric techniques are applied to a bivariate vector autoregressive model using monthly observations on the IFC stock price index and the real effective exchange rate over 1985:01-1994:07. The results show unidirectional causality from exchange rates to stock prices in all the sample countries, except the Philippines. This finding has policy implications; it suggests that respective governments should be cautious in their implementation of exchange rate policies, given that such policies have ramifications on their stock markets.

MORLEY, BRUCE & PENTECOST, ERIC J (2000) investigate the nature of the relationship between stock prices and spot exchange rates using recent developments in time series XXX ode ling. We are able to explain why traditional econometric techniques show little correlation between bilateral exchange rates and stock prices. The reason is that stock prices and exchange rates do not exhibit common trends, but do exhibit common cycles. Common cycle tests are used in this paper to show this result for the G-7 countries exchange rates and relative stock market prices indices using monthly data over the period from 1982 to 1994.

KANAS, ANGELOS (2000) investigates the interdependence of stock returns and exchange rate changes within the same economy. Six countries were tested for volatility spillovers, namely the U.S., Great Britain, Japan, Germany, Canada and France. Evidence of spillovers from stock returns to exchange rate changes is found for all countries except Germany. These results suggest that the asset approach to exchange rate determination is valid when formulated in terms of the second moments of the exchange rate distribution for these countries. The spillovers from stock returns to exchange rate changes are symmetric in nature. Volatility spillovers from exchange rate changes to stock returns are insignificant for all countries.

KANAS, ANGELOS (2002) investigate whether the volatility of exchange rate changes is affected by the volatility of stock returns for three industrialized countries, namely the US, the UK and Japan. These findings suggest that the volatility of home stock returns is a significant determinant of the volatility of exchange rate changes in all three countries, supporting the validity of the asset approach models to exchange rates for the US, the UK and Japan. Moreover, these results can be interpreted as evidence that the financial markets in these countries are integrated, in line with Zapatero (1995).

GRAMBOVAS, CHRISTOS A (2003) analyzes the interaction between exchange rate fluctuations and equity prices in three European emerging financial markets, Greece, the Czech Republic and Hungary. Corporate value of firms involved in international trade, Sensitivity to exchange rate fluctuations, Long-run and short-run dynamics between stock prices and exchange rates.

Agarwal, Chakrabarti et al (2003) have found in their research that the equity return has a significant and positive impact on the FII. But given the huge volume of investments, foreign investors could play a role of market makers and book their profits, i.e., they can buy financial assets when the prices are declining thereby jacking-up the asset prices and sell when the asset prices are increasing. Hence, there is a possibility of bi-directional relationship between FII and the equity returns.

BAILEY, WARREN & BHAOPICHITR, KIRIDA (2004) study the impact of silver price changes on stock returns from seven small open economies that switched among silver, gold, and paper money standards at different times between 1873 and 1939. Silver exposure is a priced factor in monthly equity returns. Changes in silver prices forecast realized monthly equity risk premiums, suggesting that expected risk premiums varied with the price of silver. Changes in silver prices forecast annual indicators of trade flows, global business cycles, and inflation. The evidence show corporate profits and stock market risk premiums are linked to exchange rates, trade, economic activity, and inflation.

RAMASAMY, BALA & YEUNG, MATTHEW C. H (2005) consider the causality between the two markets in nine east Asian economies. Author find that the direction of causality tends to demonstrate a hit-and-run XXX ode ling and switches according to the length of period chosen. This implies that great caution should be taken when interpreting Granger causality results.

MCPHERSON, MATTHEW Q (2006) studies the link between foreign exchange and stock markets have numerous practical business implications. If international diversification strategies are to be successful, these markets should display low levels of correlation. In addition, understanding the determinants of asset volatilities, as well as their international correlations, are important parameters for the day to day risk management of financial institutions, the risk management of firms operating internationally, and the pricing of contingent claims. This paper examines whether there is a link between exchange rate stability and stock market volatility and correlations. I find that the connection between exchange rates and stock market correlations and volatilities extends beyond periods of extreme crisis.

Dhamija Nidhi (2007) held that the increase in the volume of foreign institutional investment (FII) inflows in recent years has led to concerns regarding the volatility of these flows, threat of capital flight, its impact on the stock markets and influence of changes in regulatory regimes. The determinants and destinations of these flows and how are they influencing economic development in the country have also been debated. This paper examines the role of various factors relating to individual firm-level characteristics and macroeconomic-level conditions influencing FII investment. The regulatory environment of the host country has an important impact on FII inflows. As the pace of foreign investment began to accelerate, regulatory policies have changed to keep up with changed domestic scenarios. The paper also provides a review of these changes.

KYUNG-CHUN MUN (2008) investigates the effect of exchange rate fluctuations on international stock market fundamentals including market volatility and cross-market correlations around the Asian financial crisis. Evidence presented in this paper indicates that exchange rate fluctuations contribute largely to higher equity market volatility and cross-market correlations. Falling (rising) US stock markets are associated with depreciating (appreciating) local currencies for most of the sample markets, i.e., a positive correlation between the US market returns and local currency values. Results from forecast error variance decomposition indicate that exchange rate fluctuations become more important in explaining the time series behavior of equity market volatility and cross-market correlations during the Asian financial crisis.

2.3 BACKGROUND OF THE STUDY

The foreign exchange (also known as the currency, forex or FX) market exists wherever one currency is traded for another. It is the largest and most liquid financial market in the world and includes trading between large banks, central banks, currency speculators, multinational corporations, governments, and other financial markets and institutions.

Stock markets refer to a market place where investors can buy and sell stocks. The price at which each buying and selling transaction takes is determined by the market forces (i.e. demand and supply for a particular stock).

Share markets across the world are recuperating with traces of recession still visible in few nations. The Indian stock market is fast recovering and the emerging opportunities have led to the steady inflows of foreign investments. Investing in India has thus become a trend which is likely to gain more impetus in the near future. It is the promotion oriented user friendly policies of the Indian government that have led to this sudden surge. And owing to the increased quantum of foreign investment inflows, India is emerging as one of the best performing markets.

2.4 PROBLEM STATEMENT

Generally, Foreign Exchange Market is affected by many factors like, economic, political and legal. Recently Indian Foreign Exchange Market has passed through many ups and down trends. There are a few reasons behind the volatility like, political uncertainty, surging up inflation rates, increasing interest rates and performance of various industries. **It is also possible that Foreign Exchange Market is influenced by stock indices and there are some factors which cause the fluctuations in exchange rates**. For that we want to analyze whether Indian stock market significantly affects the foreign exchange rate or not and also see the impact of FIIs in Indian stock market.

Research Problem: Is there any impact of FOREX & FIIs in S&P CNX DEFTY?

2.5 OBJECTIVES OF THE STUDY

- To find out whether foreign exchange rate and stock market are linked

- To find out the degree of correlation between these two phenomena

- To analyze the impact of FIIs in Indian stock market as well as it's indirect impact on Foreign Exchange Rate

2.6 RESEARCH METHODOLOGY

Research methodology is the arrangement of conditions for collection and analysis of data in a manner that aims to combine relevance to the research purpose with economy in procedure. Research methodology is the conceptual structure within which research is conducted. It constitutes the blueprint for the collection measurement and analysis of the data.

The research methodology here includes:

2.6.1 Research design

2.6.2 Data collection method

2.6.3 Type of Research

2.6.4 Research Analysis Tools

2.6.5 Hypothesis

3.1   RESEARCH DESIGN

➢ SAMPLING

We have considered last **60 months** from **January 2007 to December 2011** as our research sample because this period covers Boom, Recession and Recovery of Indian economy and we have also seen the effects of decoupling of Indian stock market from various leading stock markets of the world. For that we have been using USD for foreign exchange rate, S&P CNX Defty for the stock market and FII data.

3.2 DATA COLLECTION METHOD

Secondary data: Data collection is the selection of sources of information and selection of methods and procedures for gathering data needed for any research work. "The search for answers to research questions is called collection of Data". Data are facts and other relevant materials serving as basses for study and analysis.

Basically there are two sources of data collection:-

   1. Primary sources   2. Secondary sources

For my study purpose I have used Secondary sources

For the secondary data various literatures, books, journals, magazines, web links are used. As there are not possibilities of collecting data personally so no questionnaire is made.

3.3 TYPE OF RESEARCH

As an **exploratory study** is conducted with an objective **to gain familiarity with the phenomenon** or to achieve new insight into it, this study aims to find the new insights in terms of finding the relationship between Exchange Rate and Indian Stock Indices.

3.4 RESEARCH ANALYSIS TOOLS

> **Regression Analysis:**

We can analyze how a single dependent variable is affected by the values of one or more independent variables — for example, how an athlete's performance is affected by such factors as age, height, and weight. We can apportion shares in the performance measure to each of these three factors, based on a set of performance data, and then use the results to predict the performance of a new, untested athlete.

> **Correlation:**

This analysis tool and its formulas measure the relationship between two data sets that are scaled to be independent of the unit of measurement. The population correlation calculation returns the covariance of two data sets divided by the product of their standard deviations. We can use the Correlation tool to determine whether two ranges of data move together that is, whether large values of one set are associated with large values of the other (positive correlation), whether small values of one set are associated with large values of the other (negative correlation), or whether values in both sets are unrelated (correlation near zero).

3.5 <u>HYPOTHESIS</u>

Hypothesis is usually considered as the principal instrument in Research. Its main function is to suggest new experiments and observations. In fact, many experiments are carried out with the deliberate object of testing hypothesis.

✓ <u>**Null Hypothesis:-**</u>

H_O: There is no relationship between foreign exchange rate and S&P CNX DEFTY.

H_O: There is no impact of FIIs in S&P CNX DEFTY.

✓ <u>**Alternative Hypothesis:-**</u>

H_1: There is relationship between foreign exchange rate and S&P CNX DEFTY.

H_1: There is impact of FIIs in S&P CNX DEFTY.

2.7 SCOPE AND NEED OF THE STUDY

Scope of the study is very broader and covers both the S&P CNX Defty and its comparison with foreign exchange rate. The time period is limited from January 2007 to December 2011 as it will give exact impact in both the bullish and bearish   trend.

The study will provide a very clear picture of the impact of S&P CNX Defty on Foreign Exchange Rate. It will also describe the market trends due to FIIs inflow and outflow.

The study would be helpful for further descriptive studies on the ideas that will be explored. Moreover, it would be beneficial to gain knowledge regarding foreign exchange market, FIIs and S&P CNX Defty.

2.8 LIMITATION OF STUDY

Besides following scientific methodologies the study has come across some limitations:

- The study is conducted on the basis of only 5 years data.
- Secondary data that we have used in this study may not give true picture of the concern.
- Other subjective factors have not been considered.

PART 3. DATA ANALYSIS AND INTERPRETATION

The sample data consists of 60 months' observations for FII, S&P CNX Defty and Foreign Exchange Rate (USD/INR) starting from January 2007 to December 2011. This time period consist of recession and recovery state of situation. FII was taken as independent variable. S&P CNX Defty and Foreign Exchange Rate were taken as dependent variable. The data was taken from various financial sites.

The relationship among these three variables is studied for the year 2007 & 2011 with the help of correlation and regression analysis. The results and the analysis are shown below:

3.1 CORRELATIONS

Correlation

Correlation is a statistical technique that can show whether and how strongly pairs of variables are related. For example, height and weight are related; taller people tend to be heavier than shorter people. The relationship isn't perfect. People of the same height vary in weight, and you can easily think of two people you know where the shorter one is heavier than the taller one. Nonetheless, the average weight of people 5'5" is less than the average weight of people 5'6", and their average weight is less than that of people 5'7", etc. Correlation can tell you just how much of the variation in peoples' weights is related to their heights.

Although this correlation is fairly obvious your data may contain unsuspected correlations. You may also suspect there are correlations, but don't know which are the strongest. An intelligent correlation analysis can lead to a greater understanding of your data.

Techniques in Determining Correlation

There are several different correlation techniques. The Survey System's optional Statistics Module includes the most common type, called the Pearson or product-moment correlation. The module also includes a variation on this type called partial correlation. The latter is useful when you want to look at the relationship between two variables while removing the effect of one or two other variables.

Like all statistical techniques, correlation is only appropriate for certain kinds of data. **Correlation works for quantifiable data** in which numbers are meaningful, usually quantities of some sort. It cannot be used for purely categorical data, such as gender, brands purchased, or favorite color.

Rating Scales

Rating scales are a controversial middle case. The numbers in rating scales have meaning, but that meaning isn't very precise. They are not like quantities. With a quantity (such as dollars), the difference between 1 and 2 is exactly the same as between 2 and 3. With a rating scale, that isn't really the case. You can be sure that your respondents think a rating of 2 is between a rating of 1 and a rating of 3, but you cannot be sure they think it is exactly halfway between. This is especially true if you labeled the mid-points of your scale (you cannot assume "good" is exactly half way between "excellent" and "fair").

Most statisticians say you cannot use correlations with rating scales, because the mathematics of the technique assume the differences between numbers are exactly equal. Nevertheless, many survey researchers do use correlations with rating scales, because the results usually reflect the real world. Our own position is that you can use correlations with rating scales, but you should do so with care. When working with quantities, correlations provide precise measurements. When working with rating scales, correlations provide general indications.

Correlation Coefficient

The main result of a correlation is called the **correlation coefficient** (or "r"). It ranges from -1.0 to +1.0. The closer r is to +1 or -1, the more closely the two variables are related.

If r is close to 0, it means there is no relationship between the variables. If r is positive, it means that as one variable gets larger the other gets larger. If r is negative it means that as one gets larger, the other gets smaller (often called an "inverse" correlation).

While correlation coefficients are normally reported as r = (a value between -1 and +1), squaring them makes then easier to understand. The square of the coefficient (or r square) is equal to the percent of the variation in one variable that is related to the variation in the other. After squaring r, ignore the decimal point. An r of .5 means 25% of the variation is related (.5 squared =.25). An r value of .7 means 49% of the variance is related (.7 squared = .49).

A correlation report can also show a second result of each test - statistical significance. In this case, the significance level will tell you how likely it is that the correlations reported may be due to chance in the form of random sampling error. If you are working with small sample sizes, choose a report format that includes the significance level. This format also reports the sample size.

A key thing to remember when working with correlations is never to assume a correlation means that a change in one variable causes a change in another. Sales of personal computers and athletic shoes have both risen strongly in the last several years and there is a high correlation between them, but you cannot assume that buying computers causes people to buy athletic shoes (or vice versa).

The second caveat is that the Pearson correlation technique works best with linear relationships: as one variable gets larger, the other gets larger (or smaller) in direct proportion. It does not work well with curvilinear relationships (in which the relationship does not follow a straight line). An example of a **curvilinear relationship** is age and health care. They are related, but the relationship doesn't follow a straight line. Young children and older people both tend to use much more health care than teenagers or young adults. Multiple regression (also included in the Statistics Module) can be used to examine curvilinear relationships, but it is beyond the scope of this article.

Calculating the Correlation

Now we're ready to compute the correlation value. The formula for the correlation is:

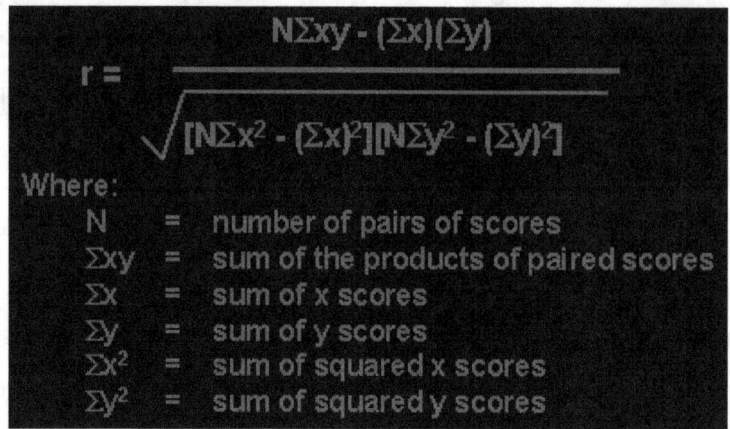

$$r = \frac{N\Sigma xy - (\Sigma x)(\Sigma y)}{\sqrt{[N\Sigma x^2 - (\Sigma x)^2][N\Sigma y^2 - (\Sigma y)^2]}}$$

Where:

N	=	number of pairs of scores
Σxy	=	sum of the products of paired scores
Σx	=	sum of x scores
Σy	=	sum of y scores
Σx^2	=	sum of squared x scores
Σy^2	=	sum of squared y scores

We use the symbol **r** to stand for the correlation. Through the magic of mathematics it turns out that r will always be between -1.0 and +1.0. if the correlation is negative, we have a negative relationship; if it's positive, the relationship is positive.

3.2 REGRESSION

Regression Definition:

A regression is a statistical analysis assessing the association between two variables. It is used to find the relationship between two variables.

Regression Formula:

Regression Equation(y) = a + bx

Slope (b) = (NΣXY - (ΣX)(ΣY)) / (NΣX2 - (ΣX)2)

Intercept (a) = (ΣY - b (ΣX)) / N

Where

   X and y are the variables.

   b = The slope of the regression line

   a = The intercept point of the regression line and the y axis.

   N = Number of values or elements

   X = First Score

   Y = Second Score

   ΣXY = Sum of the product of first and Second Scores

   ΣX = Sum of First Scores

   ΣY = Sum of Second Scores

   ΣX2 = Sum of square First Scores

LINEAR REGRESSION:

From above calculation it is interpreted that if there is change of 1 unit of S&P CNX Defty, there are chances of movement in exchange rate by %

FOREX DATA (Table-1.1)

Month	USD/INR	Month	USD/INR
Mar-07	43.79	Sep-09	48.29
Jun-07	40.59	Dec-09	46.52
Sep-07	40.17	Mar-10	45.45
Dec-07	39.37	Jun-10	46.49
Mar-08	40.15	Sep-10	45.87
Jun-08	42.76	Dec-10	45.1
Sep-08	45.53	Mar-11	44.91
Dec-08	48.51	Jun-11	46.81
Mar-09	51.13	Sep-11	47.69
Jun-09	47.67	Dec-11	52.38

(Chart-1.1)

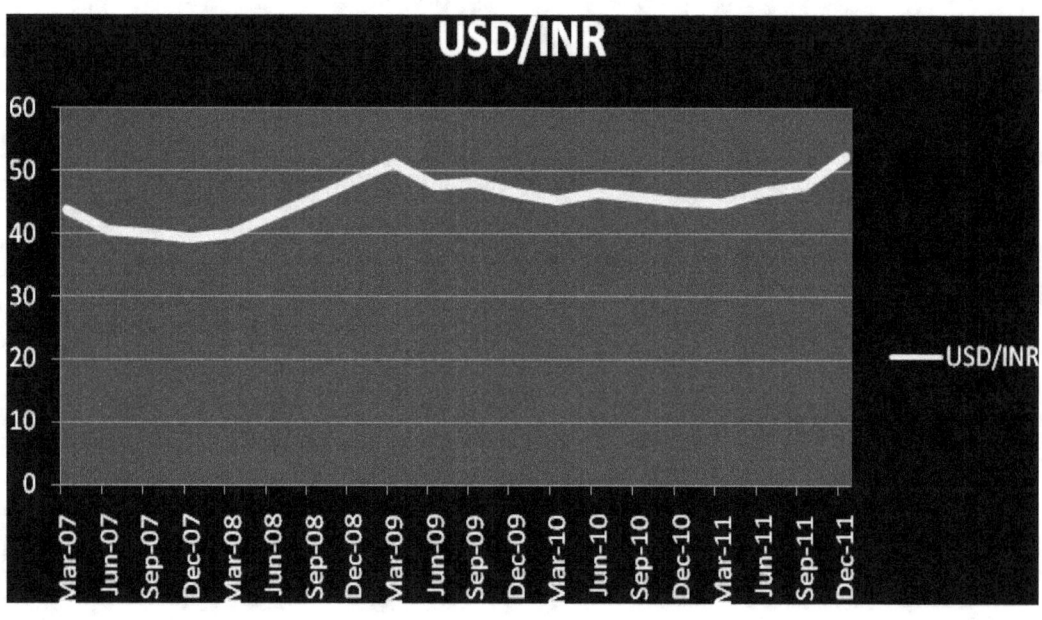

S&P CNX DEFTY DATA (Table-1.2)

Month	USD/IND	Month	USD/IND
Mar-07	2937.2	Sep-09	3776.3
Jun-07	3588.7	Dec-09	3791.1
Sep-07	4006.1	Mar-10	3944.0
Dec-07	5246.6	Jun-10	3860.2
Mar-08	4097.3	Sep-10	4380.3
Jun-08	3612.6	Dec-10	4585.1
Sep-08	3198.4	Mar-11	4266.2
Dec-08	2064.3	Jun-11	4228.1
Mar-09	1896.4	Sep-11	3646.8
Jun-09	3216.7	Dec-11	3149.2

(Chart-1.2)

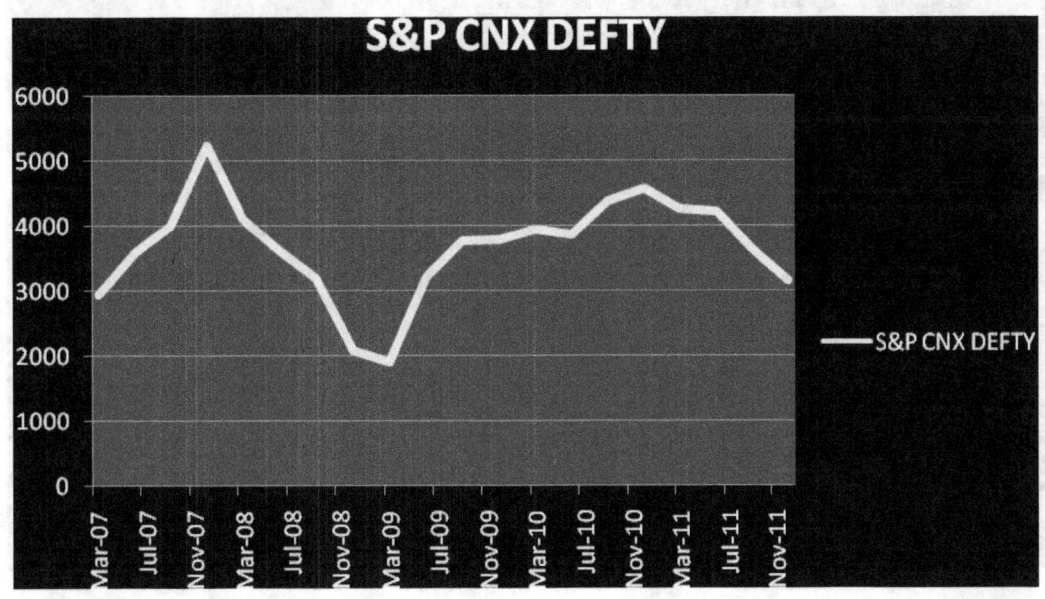

FII DATA (Table-1.3)

Month	Rs. In Crore	Month	Rs. In Crore
Mar-07	360.60	Sep-09	20,572.70
Jun-07	1,101.70	Dec-09	8,710.70
Sep-07	18,788.40	Mar-10	29,437.50
Dec-07	8,891.10	Jun-10	11,249.10
Mar-08	-1,010.10	Sep-10	32,668.00
Jun-08	-11,094.50	Dec-10	3,213.80
Sep-08	-5,073.90	Mar-11	6,882.90
Dec-08	2,376.60	Jun-11	4,883.30
Mar-09	-5,890.00	Sep-11	-1,865.70
Jun-09	4,898.30	Dec-11	0

(Chart-1.3)

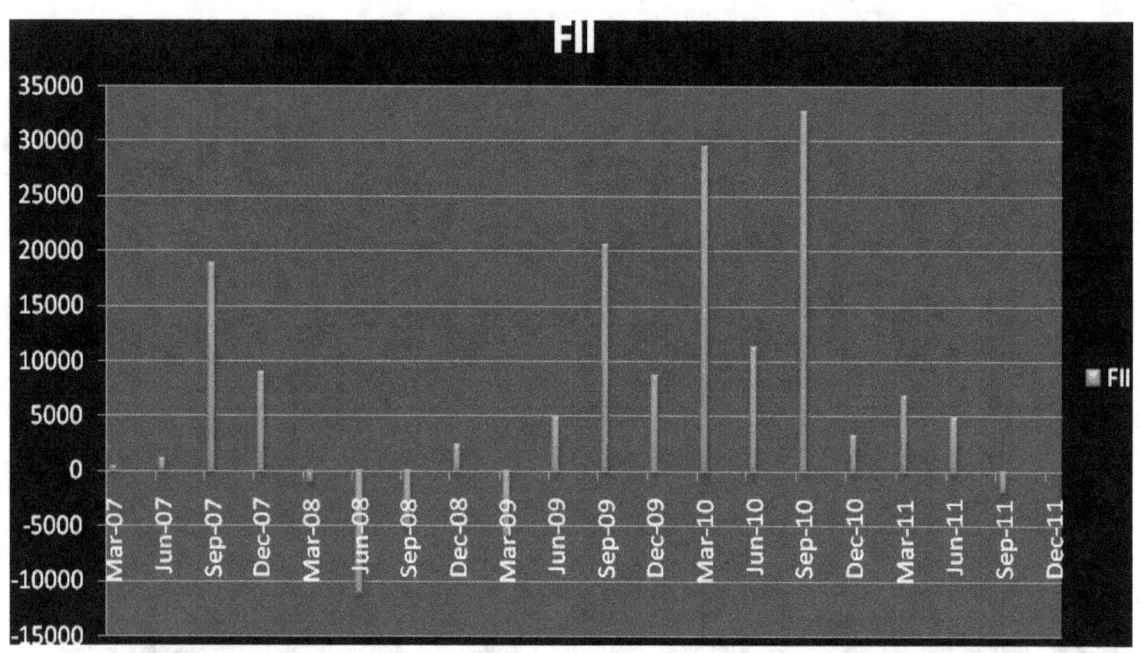

CORRELATION BETWEEN FOREX AND S&P CNX DEFTY (Chart-1.4)

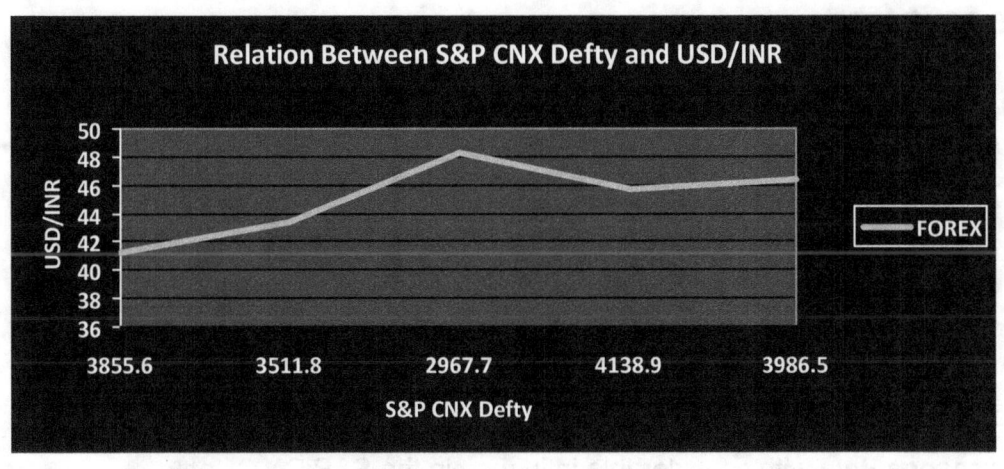

Relation Between S&P CNX Defty and USD/INR

Descriptive Statistics (Table-1.4)

	Mean	Std. Deviation	N	Correlation
USD/INR	44.997	3.318	60	-0.629
DEFTY	3692.14	796.98	60	

Correlations (Table-1.5)

		USD	S & P
USD/INR	Pearson Correlation	1	-.629(**)
	Sig. (2-tailed)		.000
	Sum of Squares and Cross-products	649.600	-98170.496
	Covariance	11.010	-1663.907
	N	60	60
S & P CNX DEFTY	Pearson Correlation	-.629(**)	1
	Sig. (2-tailed)	.000	
	Sum of Squares and Cross-products	-98170.496	37475782.270
	Covariance	-1663.907	635182.750
	N	60	60

** Correlation is significant at the 0.01 level (2-tailed).

INTERPRITATION:

H_o: **IS REJECTED**

There is negative relationship between foreign exchange rate and S&P CNX DEFTY

There is inverse relationship between Foreign Exchange Rate and S&P CNX Defty in absolute term so increase in Defty leads to decrease in foreign exchange rate, means Rupee gets depreciated and consequently the value of Rupee decreases against Dollar. This means that S&P CNX Defty has a relation with Exchange Rate with considerable influence in the S&P CNX Defty.

In the fiscal 2008-09, the Rupee depreciated against major international currencies, except pound sterling, due to deceleration in capital flows and widening trade deficit. The annual average exchange rate was Rs 45.99 per US dollar indicating depreciation by 12.5% in 2008-09 over the annual average exchange rate in 2007-08.

The Rupee depreciation during 2008-09 reflected mainly the supply-demand imbalance in the foreign exchange market, which widened significantly during September-October 2008, as fallout of the global crisis. After the fall of the Lehman Brothers in September 2008, the decline in the Rupee became more pronounced.

This led RBI to augment supply of US dollars to stabilize the Rupee in the foreign exchange market. In the fiscal 2009-10, with the signs of recovery and return of foreign institutional investments (FIIs) flows after March 2009, Rupee has again been strengthening against US dollar. The month-to-month movement of exchange rate in the year 2009-10 indicated that the Rupee appreciated against the US dollar within the range of 0.3% to 3.7% during April 2009 to December 2009, except July, September and December 2009, when Rupee depreciated by 1.5%, 0.3% and 0.13% respectively. On month-on-month basis, the average monthly exchange rate of the Rupee strengthened to Rs 50.03 per US dollar in April 2009 vis-a-vis the average rate of Rs 51.23 per US dollar during March 2009, indicating 2.4% appreciation.

However, during the month of December 2009, the average monthly exchange rate weakened to Rs 46.63 per US dollar, reflecting marginal depreciation of 0.13% over average exchange rate of Rs 46.57 per US dollar during November 2009, mainly on account of strengthening of US dollar in the international market.

The sharp depreciation of the rupee against the US dollar has resulted in foreign exchange losses worth Rs 4,800 crore for companies in the nifty index during the second quarter of 2011-12.

According to a study conducted by Crisil Research this represents one of the highest aggregate forex losses in a single quarter, given the sharp rupee depreciation and nearly threefold rise in foreign debt of these firms in five years.

"Due to a further 8% depreciation of the rupee against the dollar in 2011-12 quarter, these companies are likely to report further foreign exchange losses of nearly 35-40 billion in the quarter, assuming there are no major changes in hedging policies of individual companies," said Prasad Koparkar, head of industry and customised research at Crisil Research.

In the three months to September, these firms suffered forex loss of 4,800 crore. In July-December, the Indian currency depreciated nearly 18% against the greenback.

Sectors such as oil refining and marketing, telecom, and steel are likely to bear most of the brunt, as over one-fourth of the debt of companies in these sectors is foreign currency denominated. Also, raw materials, including crude oil are bought in dollars, thus adding to the cost burden.

The cumulative foreign currency debt of the 42 Nifty companies analysed was estimated at 1.5 lakh crore, or around 24% of the firms' total outstanding debt.

REGRESSION ANALYSIS OF S&P CNX DEFTY AND USD/INR

Variables Entered/Removed (b) (Table-1.6)

Model	Variables Entered	Variables Removed	Method
1	S&P CNX DEFTY(a)	.	Enter

a All requested variables entered.
b Dependent Variable: USD/INR

Model Summary (Table-1.7)

Model	R	R Square	Adjusted R Square	Std. Error of the Estimate
1	.629(a)	.396	.385	2.60118

a Predictors: (Constant), S&P CNX DEFTY

ANOVA (b) (Table-1.8)

Model		Sum of Squares	Df	Mean Square	F	Sig.
1	Regression	257.165	1	257.165	38.008	.000(a)
	Residual	392.435	58	6.766		
	Total	649.600	59			

a Predictors: (Constant), S&P CNX DEFTY
b Dependent Variable: USD/INR

Coefficients (a) (Table-1.9)

Model		Unstandardized Coefficients		Standardized Coefficients	T	Sig.
		B	Std. Error	Beta	B	Std. Error
1	(Constant)	54.669	1.604		34.075	.000
	S&P CNX DEFTY	-.003	.000	-.629	-6.165	.000

a Dependent Variable: USD/INR

INTERPRETATION:

H$_0$: IS REJECTED

There is negative relationship between foreign exchange rate and S&P CNX DEFTY

Here, R square is .326 which means that Foreign exchange rate has less impact in S&P CNX DEFTY index.

The standard error comes out to be 2.601 which are lowest. This does not mean that the relation is false but the error in linear relation is low so, it indicates very less variation. The regression coefficient is 0.003 which means 3% variability in Foreign exchange rate due to independent variable S&P CNX DEFTY which is much lower than during research period.

CORRELATION BETWEEN FIIS AND S&P CNX DEFTY (Chart-1.5)

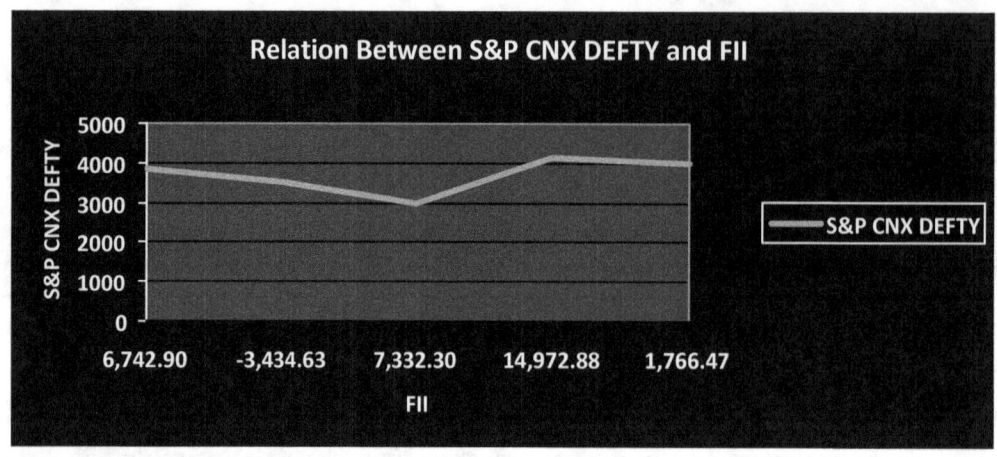

Descriptive Statistics (Table-1.10)

	Mean	Std. Deviation	N	Correlation
DEFTY	3692.14	796.98	60	0.283
FII	5414.03	10620.47	60	

Correlations (Table-1.11)

		FII	S&P CNX DEFTY
FII	Pearson Correlation	1	.283(*)
	Sig. (2-tailed)		.028
	Sum of Squares and Cross-products	6654874951.406	141331793.943
	Covariance	112794490.702	2395454.135
	N	60	60
S&P CNX DEFTY	Pearson Correlation	.283(*)	1
	Sig. (2-tailed)	.028	
	Sum of Squares and Cross-products	141331793.943	37475782.270
	Covariance	2395454.135	635182.750
	N	60	60

* Correlation is significant at the 0.05 level (2-tailed).

INTERPRETATION:

H$_o$: IS REJECTED

There is positive relationship between FIIs and S&P CNX DEFTY

There is positive relationship between FII Flows and S&P CNX Defty but correlation is moderate. It may be due to less FII activities during recession period time and good flow in recovery as well as boom time. So, combination of both state of period may reflect moderate relationship. So, other factors may be responsible behind movement in stock indices

Looking at monthly trend in FII investments during 2008-09 and 2011, it can be seen that net FII investments have been negative in the months of the fiscal.

During 2008-09, FIIs have been net sellers to the tune of US $ 11,456 million. This can be attributed to the weak sentiments of investors, following the global credit crisis which engulfed the developed countries and is seen to be affecting the developing countries as well.

Due to The Egyptian political turmoil during January 2011, FII had pulled out huge amount of money and afterwards improvement has shown. Reason for improving FII flows might be the favourable Budget.

In 2011 Overall flows to India will be lesser due to rising oil prices, high inflation and slowing growth, India cannot command as high a market share as last year 2010.

REGRESSION ANALYSIS OF FII AND S&P CNX DEFTY

Variables Entered/ Removed (b) (Table-1.12)

Model	Variables Entered	Variables Removed	Method
1	FII(a)	.	Enter

a All requested variables entered.
b Dependent Variable: S&P CNX NEFTY

Model Summary (Table-1.13)

Model	R	R Square	Adjusted R Square	Std. Error of the Estimate
1	.283(a)	.080	.064	770.96303

a Predictors: (Constant), FII

ANOVA (b) (Table-1.14)

Model		Sum of Squares	df	Mean Square	F	Sig.
1	Regression	3001510.340	1	3001510.340	5.050	.028(a)
	Residual	34474271.93	58	594383.999		
	Total	37475782.27	59			

a Predictors: (Constant), FII
b Dependent Variable: S&P CNX NEFTY

Coefficients (a) (Table-1.15)

Model		Unstandardized Coefficients		Standardized Coefficients	t	Sig.
		B	Std. Error	Beta	B	Std. Error
1	(Constant)	3577.169	111.912		31.96	.000
	FII	.021	.009	.283	2.24	.028

A Dependent Variable: S&P CNX NEFTY

INTERPRETATION:

H$_o$: IS REJECTED

There is positive relationship between FIIs and S&P CNX DEFTY

Here we can say that effect of change of independent variable changing the dependent variable. The regression coefficient is **0.021** which reflects 21.0 % variability in S&P CNX DEFTY with the independent variable and it is low i.e. FII and how much the FII affects the S&P CNX DEFTY in 2007 to 2011. The standard error comes out to be **770.96303** which are moderate and so it means that the deviation from the mean value is very low. This does not mean the relation is false but we can say that the error in linear relation is low.

PART- 4 RESULT AND FINDINGS

(A)   Here, Foreign Exchange Rate and S&P CNX Defty having negative co-relation between them, because the co-relation is -0.629 as shown 2008-09 is depreciate **12.5%** against U.S dollar, And in 2009-10 is 0.3 % to 3.7% appreciated.

The sharp depreciation of the rupee against the US dollar has resulted in foreign exchange losses worth Rs 4,800 crore for companies in the nifty index during the second quarter of 2011-12.

(B)   The regression coefficient is 0.003 which means 3% variability in Foreign exchange rate due to independent variable S&P CNX DEFTY which is much lower than during research period.

Sectors such as oil refining and marketing, telecom, and steel are likely to bear most of the brunt, as over one-fourth of the debt of companies in these sectors is foreign currency denominated. Also, raw materials, including crude oil are bought in dollars, thus adding to the cost burden.

The cumulative foreign currency debt of the 42 Nifty companies analysed was estimated at 1.5 lakh crore, or around 24% of the firms' total outstanding debt.

(C)   There is positive relationship between FII Flows and S&P CNX Defty and correlation is moderate but many other factor are also affecting S&P CNX Defty because co-relation between FII and S&P CNX Defty is 0.283 and it is very lowest,

During 2008-09, FIIs have been net sellers to the tune of US $ 11,456 million. This can be attributed to the weak sentiments of investors, following the global credit crisis.

(D) The regression coefficient is **0.021** which reflects 21.0 % variability in S&P CNX DEFTY with the independent variable and it is lowest.

Due to The Egyptian political turmoil during January 2011, FII had pulled out huge amount of money and afterwards improvement has shown. Reason for improving FII flows might be the favourable Budget.

In 2011 Overall flows to India will be lesser due to rising oil prices, high inflation and slowing growth, India cannot command as high a market share as last year 2010.

PART- 5 CONCLUSIONS/ SUGGESTION

In developing countries like India foreign capital helps in increasing the productivity of labour and to build up foreign exchange reserves to meet the current account deficit. Foreign Investment provides a channel through which country can have access to foreign capital.

After all analysis of data it is found that there is inverse relationship between Foreign Exchange Rate and S&P CNX Defty. So, when there is upward movement in Indian stock indices, exchange rate (USD) goes down. Consequently, value of Rupee appreciates and vice versa.

According to Data analysis and findings, it can be concluded that FII do have significant impact on the Indian Stock Market but there are other factors like government policies, budgets, bullion market, inflation, economical and political condition, etc. do also have an impact on the Indian stock market. Moreover, there is direct relationship between FII flows in Indian stock market which means that when they invest in India in huge quantum , then Indian market is likely to go up and vice versa but there is moderate correlation between these two variables. So, overall it is concluded that there is weak effect of FII flows in Indian Stock market but there is moderate relation between S&P CNX Defty and Foreign Exchange Rate.

PART 6. BIBLIOGRAPHY

➢ **SOFTWARE**

SPSS (15.0 FOR Windows Evaluation Version Demo)

➢ **WEBSITES**

http://www.nseindia.com

http://www.investopedia.com

http://www.bseindia.com/about/st_key/keystats011.asp

http://www.onada.com/currency/historical-rates/

http://www.nseindia.com/content/indices/ind_histvalues.htm

http://www.sebi.gov.in/sebiweb/investment/statistics.jsp?s=fii

http://www.easycalculation.com/statistics/correlation.php

➢ **REFERENCES**

1. Abdalla, Issam S.A & Murinde, Victor (1997), **Exchange rate and stock price interactions in emerging financial markets: evidence on India, Korea, Pakistan and the Philippines,** *Applied Financial Economics, Vol. 7*

2. Ajayi, Richard A & Mougoué, Mbodja (1996), **on the dynamic relation between stock prices and exchange rates**, *Journal of Financial Research, Vol. 19*

3. Bahmani-Oskooee, Mohsen & Sohrabian, Ahmad (1992), **Stock prices and the effective exchange rate of the dollar**, *Applied Economics, Vol. 24*

4. Bailey, Warren & Bhaopichitr, Kirida (2004), **How Important Was Silver? Some Evidence on Exchange Rate Fluctuations and Stock Returns in Colonial-Era Asia,** *Journal of Business, Vol. 77*

5. Golaka C Nath and G P Samanta (2003), **Relationship Between Exchange Rate and Stock Prices in India – An Empirical Analysis,** *http://papers.ssrn.com/sol3/papers.cfm?abstract_id=475823*

6. Grambovas, Christos A (2003), **Exchange Rate Volatility and Equity Markets,** *Eastern European Economics, Vol. 41*

7. Kanas, Angelos (2000), **Volatility Spillovers Between Stock Returns and Exchange Rate Changes: International Evidence,** *Journal of Business Finance & Accounting, Vol. 27*

8. Kanas, Angelos (2002), **Is exchange rate volatility influenced by stock return volatility? Evidence from the US, the UK and Japan,** *Applied Economics Letters, Vol. 9*

9. Kyung-Chun Mun (2008), **Effects of Exchange Rate Fluctuations on Equity Market Volatility and Correlations: Evidence from the Asian Financial Crisis,** *Quarterly Journal of Finance & Accounting, Vol. 47*

10. Ma, Christopher K & G. Wenchi Kao (1990), **On exchange rate changes and stock price reactions,** *Journal of Business Finance & Accounting, Vol. 17*

11. Maghrebi, Nabil & Holmes, Mark J & Pentecost, Eric J (2006), **Are There Asymmetries in the Relationship Between Exchange Rate Fluctuations and Stock Market Volatility in Pacific Basin Countries?,** *Review of Pacific Basin Financial Markets & Policies, Vol. 9*

12. McPherson, Matthew Q (2006), **Is There a Link Between Foreign Exchange Market Stability and Stock Market Correlations? Evidence from Canada,** *Multinational Business Review, Vol. 14*

13. Morley, Bruce & Pentecost, Eric J (2000), **Common trends and cycles in G-7 countries exchange rates and stock prices,** *Applied Economics Letters, Vol.7*

14. Ramasamy, Bala & Yeung, Matthew C. H (2005), **The causality between stock returns and exchange rates: revisited,** *Australian Economic Papers, Vol. 44*

15. Smyth, R & Nandha, M (2003), **Bivariate causality between exchange rates and stock prices in South Asia**, *Applied Economics Letters, Vol. 10*

16. Tabak, Benjamin M (2006), **The Dynamic relationship between stock prices and exchange rates: Evidence for Brazil**, *International Journal of Theoretical & Applied Finance,*

17. **THE TIMES OF INDIA** Mumbai Edition- Dt: Dec 28, 2011

PART 7. ANNEXURE

USD/IND DATA (Table-1.16)

YEAR MONTH	2007	2008	2009	2010	2011
January	44.21	39.26	48.70	45.89	45.38
February	44.02	39.67	49.21	46.27	43.00
March	43.79	40.15	51.13	45.45	44.91
April	42.02	39.97	49.67	44.44	44.32
May	40.57	42.00	48.51	45.78	44.90
Jun	40.59	42.76	47.67	46.49	46.81
July	40.27	42.75	48.36	46.76	44.40
August	40.68	42.91	48.24	46.46	45.29
September	40.17	45.53	48.29	45.87	47.69
October	39.79	48.65	46.65	44.35	46.95
November	39.33	48.91	46.53	44.93	50.67
December	39.37	48.51	46.52	45.10	52.38
Total	494.81	521.07	579.48	547.79	556.7
Avg.	**41.23**	**43.42**	**48.29**	**45.64**	**46.39**

- http://www.onada.com/currency/historical-rates/

S&P CNX DEFTY DATA (Table-1.17)

YEAR MONTH	2007	2008	2009	2010	2011
January	3156.5	5069.0	2023.8	3893.1	4414.3
February	3204.5	4534.0	1982.8	3618.5	4117.6
March	2937.2	4097.3	1896.4	3944.0	4266.2
April	3248.0	4240.6	2323.0	4122.2	4558.6
May	3555.6	4132.5	2829.5	3818.8	4236.1
Jun	3588.7	3612.6	3216.7	3860.2	4228.1
July	3836.0	3336.7	3105.5	3963.7	4366.0
August	3650.9	3561.4	3275.9	4058.9	3884.0
September	4006.1	3198.4	3776.3	4380.3	3646.8
October	4785.9	2287.0	3704.8	4754.9	3559.0
November	5051.8	2008.5	3687.4	4667.2	3412.8
December	5246.6	2064.3	3791.1	4585.1	3149.2
Total	46267.8	42142.3	35613.2	49666.9	47838.7
Avg.	**3855.6**	**3511.8**	**2967.7**	**4138.9**	**3986.5**

- http://www.nseindia.com/content/indices/ind_histvalues.htm

FII DATA (Table-1.18)

YEAR / MONTH	2007	2008	2009	2010	2011
January	-1,681.90	-11,081.90	-3,443.00	8,412.60	5,363.50
February	8,195.10	4,230.10	-3,124.40	4,363.00	-3,269.80
March	360.6	-1,010.10	-5,890.00	29,437.50	6,882.90
April	7,721.50	-626.9	8,998.50	12,393.10	7,196.10
May	5,319.80	-5,174.40	17,405.80	-6,986.10	-4,276.00
Jun	1,101.70	-11,094.50	4,898.30	11,249.10	4,883.30
July	22,609.40	1,782.10	13,181.70	24,724.00	10,652.90
August	-7,162.10	46.1	4,523.30	14,686.30	-7,902.50
September	18,788.40	-5,073.90	20,572.70	32,668.00	-1,865.70
October	23,090.40	-17,205.40	15,972.60	24,302.60	3078.8
November	-6,319.20	1,616.70	6,181.40	21,210.70	-3,263.2
December	8,891.10	2,376.60	8,710.70	3,213.80	0
Total	80,914.80	-41,215.50	87,987.60	179,674.60	17480.3
Avg.	6,742.90	-3,434.63	7,332.30	14,972.88	1,766.47

- http://www.sebi.gov.in/sebiweb/investment/statistics.jsp?s=fii